WILD WORK

WHO WALKS IN SPACE?

WORKING IN SPACE

Linda Tagliaferro

www.raintreepublishers.co.uk
Visit our website to find out
more information about
Raintree books.

To order:
☎ Phone 0845 6044371
🖹 Fax +44 (0) 1865 312263
✉ Email myorders@raintreepublishers.co.uk

Customers from outside the UK please telephone +44 1865 312262

Raintree is an imprint of Capstone Global Library Limited,
a company incorporated in England and Wales having its
registered office at 7 Pilgrim Street, London, EC4V 6LB –
Registered company number: 6695582

Text © Capstone Global Library Limited 2011
First published in hardback in 2011
Paperback edition first published in 2012
The moral rights of the proprietor have been asserted.

Edited by David Andrews, Nancy Dickmann, and Rebecca
Rissman
Designed by Victoria Allen
Picture research by Liz Alexander
Leveled by Marla Conn, with Read-Ability.
Originated by Dot Gradations Ltd
Printed and bound in China by Leo Paper Products

ISBN 978 1 4062 1678 3 (hardback)
15 14 13 12 11
10 9 8 7 6 5 4 3 2 1

ISBN 978 1 4062 1941 8 (paperback)
16 15 14 13 12
10 9 8 7 6 5 4 3 2 1

British Library Cataloguing in Publication Data
Tagliaferro, Linda.
  Who walks in space? : working in space. -- (Wild
work)
  1. Astronauts--Juvenile literature. 2. Space shuttles--
Juvenile literature. 3. Space stations--Juvenile
literature.
  I. Title II. Series
  629.4'5'023-dc22

Acknowledgements
The author and publisher are grateful to the following for
permission to reproduce copyright material:
Alamy pp. **5** (© Stocktrek Images, Inc.), **26** (© NASA); Corbis
pp. **6** (© Roger Ressmeyer), **7** (© Scott Andrews/Science
Faction), **10** (© NASA/Roger Ressmeyer), **11** (© NASA/
Reuters), **13** (© Sergei Chirikov/epa), **17**, **19**, **20** (© Bettmann),
29 (© Bettmann); Getty Images pp. **8** (Mark Wilson), **12** (Bill
Ingalls/AFP), **18** (John Nordell/Christian Science Monitor),
28 (Bruce Weaver/AFP); NASA pp. **4**, **21**, **27**; Photolibrary
pp. **23** (NASA/age footstock), **25** (White); Reuters p. **15**
(NASA); Science Photo Library pp. **9** (NASA), **14** (Detlev Van
Ravenswaay), **16** (NASA), **22** (NASA), **24** (NASA).

Background design features reproduced with permission of
© CORBIS. Cover photograph reproduced with permission
of Shutterstock (© trucic).

Contents

Teamwork in space

5, 4, 3, 2, 1... lift off! A **space shuttle** roars high into the sky. Exploring space is exciting. But it can also be very dangerous.

Many people work together to **launch** a space shuttle. Then **astronauts** can live and work safely in space.

Launching a space shuttle

People who work in **ground control** help **astronauts** take off and land. They make sure everything is safe before they **launch**, or take off. They check if bad weather is on the way.

DID YOU KNOW?

Thousands of people work together in ground control.

If there are problems, ground control stops the launch. They make sure all problems are fixed so that the astronauts are safe.

The commander

Before a **space shuttle** is **launched**, the commander makes sure the crew is well trained.

commander

In space the commander leads the crew. The commander also lands the space shuttle when it returns to Earth.

The pilot

The **pilot** sits next to the commander on the **space shuttle**. He or she might fly the shuttle to the **International Space Station**, where many **astronauts** live and work.

pilot

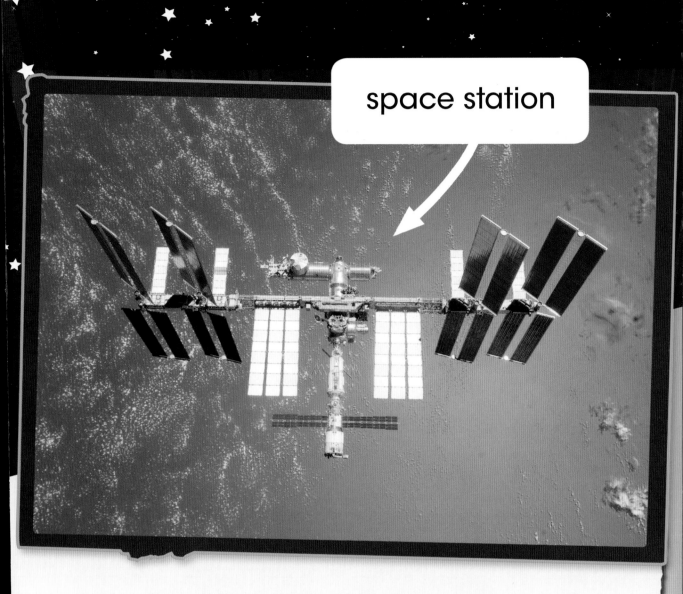

space station

The pilot **docks** the shuttle. This means the shuttle attaches to the space station. Then astronauts can safely walk into the space station.

Keeping in touch

Astronauts can live in the **International Space Station** for months. The station flies 400 kilometres (250 miles) high in an **orbit** around Earth. But they are always communicating with **ground control**. They can talk to people on the ground through a video connection.

DID YOU KNOW?
Astronauts from Britain, the USA, Russia, Canada, Japan, and other countries all work at the International Space Station.

Astronauts at work

Working in space is very different from working on Earth. **Gravity** is a force that holds things down on Earth. In space, there is little gravity. People and objects float. **Astronauts** work while floating.

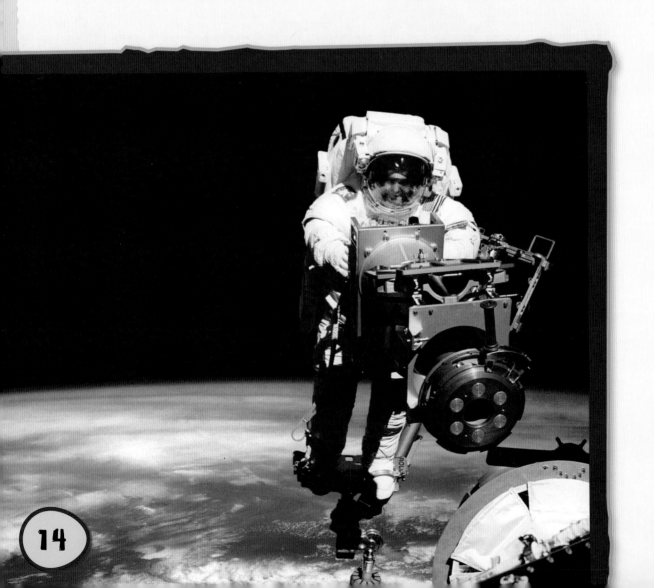

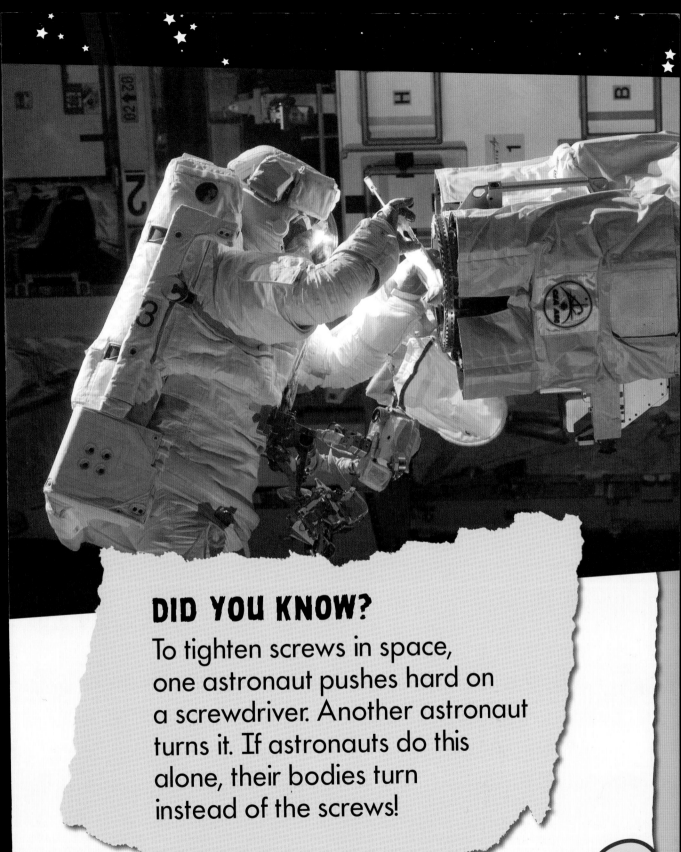

DID YOU KNOW?

To tighten screws in space, one astronaut pushes hard on a screwdriver. Another astronaut turns it. If astronauts do this alone, their bodies turn instead of the screws!

Out-of-this-world experiments

Astronauts do **experiments** to learn many things in space. They study how space affects the way plants and small animals live.

Who makes dinner in space?

For dinner, **astronauts** go to the **galley**, or kitchen. They add hot water to dry food in pouches. Some food is fresh, such as fruit.

Green Beans & Mushrooms 2/28/2005
100 mL hot water, 5-10 min
3220

Зеленая фасоль с грибами
100 мл горячей воды, 5-10 мин.

Following doctor's orders

Usually there are no doctors in space. **Astronauts** train to take care of medical problems. If they need help, they talk to a doctor on the ground.

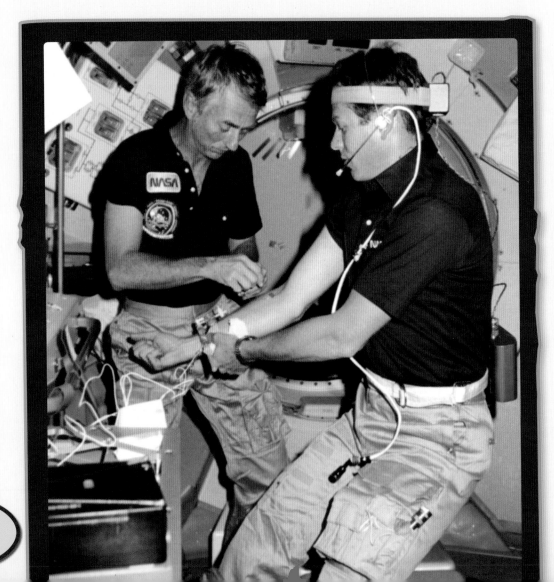

DID YOU KNOW?

Astronauts strap themselves to a treadmill to exercise. They also use machines with pedals like bicycles to use their leg muscles.

Joysticks in space

Canadarm2 is a robot "arm" on the outside of the space station. An **astronaut** looks at screens and uses a joystick to move the arm. Canadarm2 can move big pieces of equipment from one place to another.

joystick

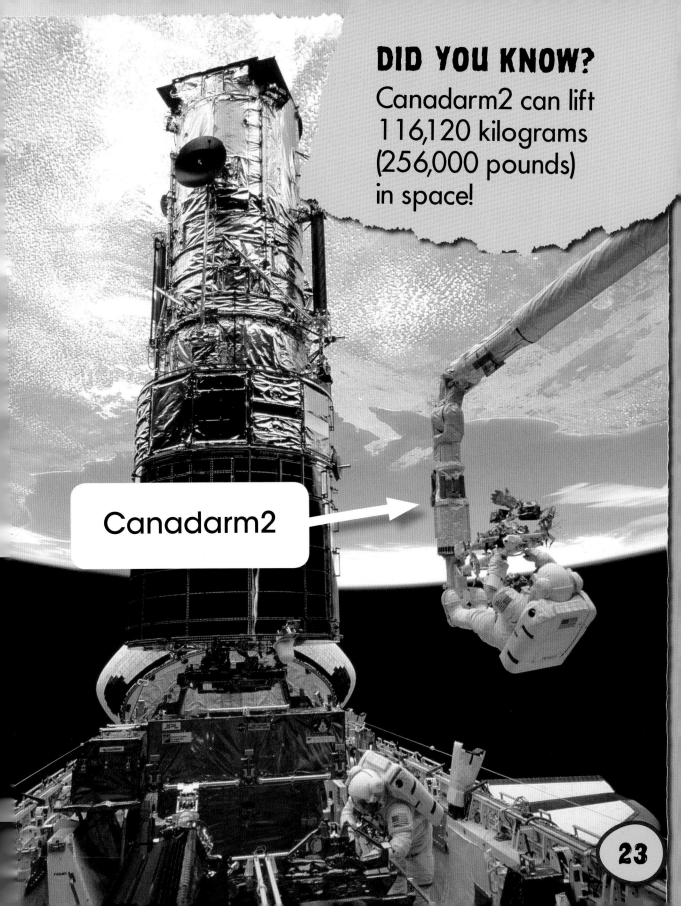

DID YOU KNOW?
Canadarm2 can lift 116,120 kilograms (256,000 pounds) in space!

Canadarm2

Walking in space

Sometimes **astronauts** walk outside the **space station**. Space has no air. It is dark and cold. One astronaut helps another into a protective suit.

DID YOU KNOW?

Just in case astronauts need to go to the toilet on a space walk, they wear a special nappy!

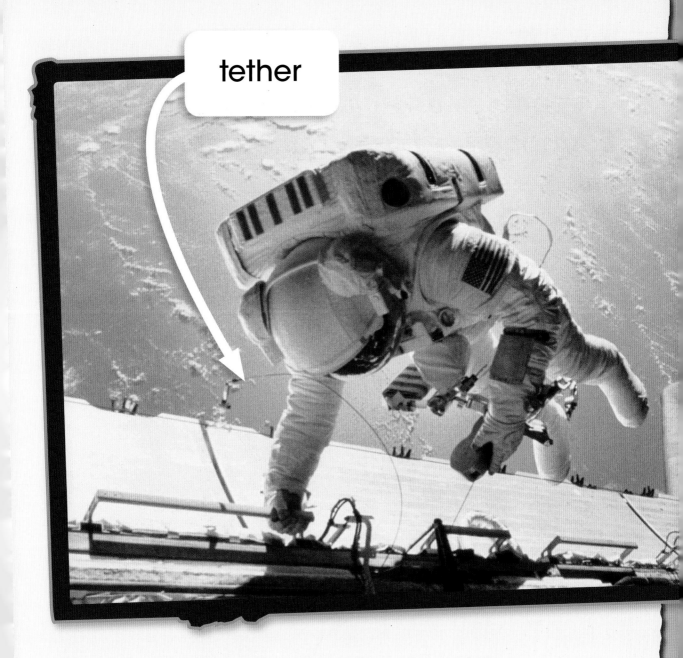

tether

Astronauts are attached to the space station by a strong rope called a **tether**.

Landing a space shuttle

A **space shuttle** circles, or **orbits**, Earth. It travels at about 28,200 kilometres (17,500 miles) per hour. That's 35 times faster than an aeroplane! To return to Earth, the commander must use controls to slow it down. The commander then lands the space shuttle like a plane.

DID YOU KNOW?

A big parachute opens behind the space shuttle when it lands. This helps to slow it down.

Could you work in space?

Would you like to explore space? To work in a space station, you must be able to make quick decisions. You need to study **astronomy**, maths, and other subjects.

Then one day, you might be looking out of a space station window. You'll smile as you see our beautiful Earth below.

Glossary

astronaut a person who goes into space

astronomy the study of space

Canadarm2 a robot arm made in Canada. It can lift heavy objects in space.

dock to land a shuttle next to the space station

experiments test done to learn something new

galley the kitchen in a space station

gravity the force that holds things down on Earth

ground control the thousands of people on the ground working to keep astronauts safe

International Space Station a space station that orbits Earth. Astronauts from many countries work there.

launch to take off from the ground

orbit to circle around the Earth in space

pilot person who steers a ship, plane, or space shuttle

space shuttle a spacecraft that can be used many times

tether a heavy rope that keeps astronauts attached to the space station when they walk in space

Find out more

Books to read

Living in Space, Patricia Whitehouse (Heinemann Library, 2005)

See Inside Space, Katie Daynes (Usborne, 2008)

Working in Space, Patricia Whitehouse (Heinemann Library, 2005)

Websites to visit

www.kidsastronomy.com/space_shuttle.htm
Learn about spaces shuttles and all their different parts.

http://iss.jaxa.jp/kids/en/life/index.html
Get answers to your questions about eating, sleeping, and more in space.

http://www.spacecentre.co.uk
Visit the National Space Centre in Leicester or go to its website to find out more about space and astronauts.

Index